THE CAT IN THE
TREBLE CLEF

Louis de Bernières

THE CAT IN THE
TREBLE CLEF

ILLUSTRATED BY DONALD SAMMUT

Harvill *Secker*

LONDON

1 3 5 7 9 10 8 6 4 2

Harvill Secker, an imprint of Vintage,
20 Vauxhall Bridge Road,
London SW1V 2SA

Harvill Secker is part of the Penguin Random House group of companies
whose addresses can be found at global.penguinrandomhouse.com

Penguin
Random House
UK

First published by Harvill Secker in 2018

A CIP catalogue record for this book is available from the British Library

penguin.co.uk/vintage

ISBN 9781787300187

Typeset in 11/15 pt Dante MT
by Integra Software Services Pvt. Ltd, Pondicherry

Printed and bound in Great Britain by Clays Ltd, Elcograf S.p.A.

Penguin Random House is committed to a sustainable future
for our business, our readers and our planet. This book is
made from Forest Stewardship Council® certified paper.

For Victoria

CONTENTS

THE ONLY ROAD THERE WAS

It was you and me. Your mother had left,
And wouldn't allow us to take the girl,
As if you can own a child, as if it were nothing
To be a father, be a brother, loving a daughter,
Loving a sister.

And you were four years old, perplexed, confused,
An innocent boy on the boat from Doolin Pier.
It was you and me, struck down by disaster;
The passage made you sick.

Out on the island we hired a trap.
There was only one road, to right or left,
The pony was expert, the driver redundant.
We rattled off, up the only road there was.

We stopped on a hilltop, wandered away
In fields squared out by sag-bulged drystone walls.
The wind soughed, the grass whispered, the sea sparkled,
The boats in the distance as small as toys,
The Atlantic sun benign on a couch of clouds.

Amongst the burrows and stones
You found hundreds of shells of beautiful snails,
Golden yellow or striped in white and brown;
You gathered them up, this fabulous treasure,

And crammed them deep in our pockets,
While back on the lane the man with the pony waited
To take us back down to the sea, on the only
    road there was.

You ate fish fingers, I ate lobster,
You drank orange, I drank wine,
Father and son, side by side in the only place to eat.
Then down on the beach you gathered shells,
Threw stones in the sea till the tide changed,
And the *Rose of Aran* returned.

I was sorting through your outgrown clothes
And found your shells in a tiny coat, and it all came back;
Buying a claddagh in Galway town,
Fashioned in silver, to leave to you in my will;
Buying a fiddle you knew how to play
The moment it came from the box;
Chasing the seagulls, eating sarnies in cafés;
Riding for miles in Connemara,
Down on the beaches, you on the cob,
    me on the hunter.

And every night I'd carry you up and put you to bed
Without your sister beside you. I'd sit at the foot,
And tell you stories of how you went up in the clouds,
And went to the moon with Sophie,
    and looked at the cats,
Because that's where they go when they die.

I have some snaps the driver took
Of you and me, collecting shells, on Inishmore,
A few miles up the only road there was.

SWIMMING WITH ROBIN IN BODRUM, 2007

A whole week in the water, with you
      attached to my neck,
Two years old, too scared to let go.
The sea was too big, the sun too close,
And even for Yasmin you wouldn't swim,
But cried and clung to her long brown arms.

Oglum, oglum, my son, my son.

Monastic ruins on grey rock,
Splashes of scarlet on every hill;
You pointed them out, said, 'Turkish flag!'

The women filled you with chocolate
That travelled all over your cheeks.
With small bare hands
You crammed your mouth with rice.

Oglum, oglum, my son, my son.

The press reported your blond hair,
Your sky-blue eyes, your apple cheeks,
And told the Turks who hadn't seen you yet,

That you were by far the most beautiful boy
Of all the boys in the world.

Oglum, oglum, my son, my son.

After all these years, they remember you still,
Your floppy hat pulled down on your head;
A whole short week in the water, holding
    hard to my neck,
Too scared to let go,
The sea too big, the sun too close.

Oglum, oglum, my son, my son.

We taught you Turkish words:
Akdeniz, *patlican, balik, su,*
Merhaba Fevzi Bey,
Merhaba Avram Bey,
Merhaba Ulker,
Merhaba Livaneli.

Since then you've learned to swim alone,
And it's evident now that all my life with you
Is one steep, painful path of letting go,
Of letting you live without me,
Of teaching you how to leave me,
The one misfortune I cannot want,

That will do the most to grieve me.
Oglum, oglum, my son, my son.
For one week the most beautiful boy
In the world, attached to my neck in Bodrum.

Note: Oglum is pronounced 'oloom'.

THE SUBSTITUTION

For Sophie, August 2008

The worst summer for years;
It has rained daily, there's
Mould on the cheek of the apple,
No grape on the vine,
No damson, no plum on the trees.
The roses have blackened,
Chickweed and horseflies thrive.

But you arrived, my tiny girl,
And pitched your patchwork tent in life,
Child of winter, daughter of snow;
And here, in the dark days of August,
Just six months old, in the tedious rain,
In the twilights at noon, now see what you've done!

The light of your laughter, the light of your face,
Replace the lost light of the sun.

FOR SOPHIE, AGED NEARLY SIX

She does the splits in three excruciating ways;
She cartwheels from a standing start;
She loves her brother, punches and kicks him,
And then she draws him pictures for his pleasure.

She stamps her feet and screams;
Wears nothing but pink; climbs trees
In princess costume, tiara and cloak,
With nothing but skin on her feet.

She puts on music, dances and tumbles
In front of mirrors, pirouettes, prances;
She leaps from the top of the stairs, cries out,
Delighted, laughing, lands in my arms.

She circles my legs, attempts to lift me;
She wins at races, leaving her elders behind.
She wakes in the morning, rounds her eyes,
Says, 'Daddy, Daddy, I dreamed I was flying.'

DRINKING ALONE IN SUMMER

Out on the terrace in August,
I fill my glass from the jug
And try to examine the stars;
But wine has increased their number,
They won't stand still for the count.
I drink their health, and I
Drink to the health of the moon.

Here's to the moth at the lamp,
Here's to the fox on the prowl,
And here's to the bats and owls
Who can't sup wine for themselves.
Never mind, my brothers,
I have a plan: I'll drink your share.
How good to you I am.

And here's to the Queen
And Pavarotti's ghost,
Segovia's too,
And many other things
I love but can't recall.

I notice my shadow, multiplied by lamps,
And see, after all, I'm hardly alone
There must be six of us at least.

My shadows and I, we raise our glass and drink.
Here's to us, what splendid friends we are.
Let's dance, be careful, let's not spill wine,
It shouldn't be wasted on stones.

It's not much good, this Grecian dance,
We've banged our knee on the bench,
We failed to hold each other up.
Let's sing instead.
I'd play guitar, but how's that done
When one hand wields a jug?
Let's bawl out something French.

Here's to the parched-up flowers and lawn,
Here's to the prospect of rain.
A soupçon more? I bow and ask myself,
Most courteously and kind.
Just one more glass perhaps.
Let's stand, good shadows!
I'd make a speech, but I'm shamefully
Short of words. I'll just propose a toast.

Here's health to my empty rooms,
The children who used to be here.

JACKDAWS AND ROOKS

We came to the end of the lane, the children and I,
In a gale that tested the trees, doubled them over,
Dotted the sky with the flutter of leaves,
Tiny rags of former life that skittered and whirled,
Torn away from the ash and the oak,
Their first ascent in the long flight
That leads at length to earth.

We skirted a branch that lay on the road,
We came to the end, we saw them then.
I stopped the car. We laughed with
Delight. The valley was gleaming,
The river wound through a channel of light
In the darkening green of the marsh.

And all above, from end to end, exploiting the lift,
The sky was crammed with a wheeling and turning,
A hurling and flinging, a tumbling and soaring
Of hundreds of thousands of jackdaws and rooks,
Riding the currents, ascending and swerving.
Out in the gale for the wind's gift.

Rejoicing in jackdaws and rooks rejoicing,
My daughter climbed over, my son made room,
Whilst I was reminded, learned again:
Go out in the gale; stretch out your wings;
Seize the day; fly in the tempest for fun.

Waveney Valley, November 2013, on
the way to Sophie's ballet class

BLACKTHORN BLOSSOM

It was blackthorn blossom drifting, blowing
   across the lane,
This springtime snow that blots against the mud,
This springtime snow that paints our coats
And settles on these stones.
My little gleeful son jumps in puddles, splashes,
Asks questions, sings his songs, demands to be carried,
Looks forward to biscuits, asks about flowers and bones.
And where is my daughter, and where is her mother,
As bluebells flower, the primrose, the kingcup,
As springtime snow, blackthorn blossom drifting,
Covers the new nettles, settles on these stones?

EVERY OTHER WEEKEND

We recognise each other. We are unmistakeable;
The ones who were deserted,
Robbed, betrayed, broken in the soul,
The ones who made a mess,
Got messed around;
We stand forlornly, hunched by the slides,
Pushing the swings too high.

Much too jolly by half,
We bravely join in, casting our pebbles out in the sea.
We observe each other and nod,
Exchange our stories in playgrounds and parks.
We have knives through our hearts, our guts torn out
And burned in front of our eyes.

We buy them ice cream,
We hug them too hard, sniff at their hair, kiss their skin,
    tickle their feet.
We hand them back on Sunday night, and then
Go homeless to silent rooms,
The cowed, defeated, disenfranchised, disjusticed men.

EMPTY VESSEL

My soul is an empty vessel; with what shall I fill it?
With women? With music? With love?
With imperishable art?
I am weary of all these things, and they are weary of me.

I remember when God walked in, stayed
    for a while, departed,
Left no card, no number, no forwarding address.
I wonder where He went, so pointedly closing the door,
Making quite sure of the click of the latch,
His feet on the gravel, the meticulous click,
The counter-click of the gate. I don't blame Him,
It was me that sent Him away,
It was me that grew faithless,
It was me that told Him to leave.

My soul is an empty vessel; with what shall I fill it?
With music? With women? With pride?

And then they come, my son, my daughter.
I hear their scrape at the door;
I leap from my chair, gather them in,
Tend to their games, their pains, their strange obsessions,
Their insatiable need to be carried and kissed.

The rooms of the house grow bright,
The grass of the lawn wakes up,
The apple tree braces its boughs.

This being so, my heart being full,
To hell with my empty soul.

THE INSPIRATION

An aspiring composer, he is often inspired by dreams,
And accordingly leaves a pad and pen
Beside the clock at night, on the table next to his bed.
He dreams one night of music, honey to the ears,
Ineffable, sublime, exquisite, music of the spheres,
Quintessence of beauty. It is 3 a.m.

He shakes himself awake, takes up the pad and pen,
And writes his lovely music down.
He goes to the bathroom, returns to bed,
Returns to the bosom of sleep.

Morning strikes and he rolls from the bed,
Looks down and rubs his chin,
Thinks, 'How did I come up with that?'
For there they are, the whiskers, the ears and eyes.
The staves are bare, but the treble clef is
Deftly redrawn as a cat.

A BOX OF OLD PHOTOGRAPHS

These are those my mother loved,
Holding furled umbrellas,
Leaning on obsolescent cars,
These their simulacra,
Shadows trapped for a time,
With tentative grins,
Self-deprecating smiles,
Quizzical eyebrows raised
On pale faces framed by hats and scarves and ties.
Their woolly dogs lean on their legs,
And some of them squint in the sun.

And now my mother joins the well-loved ghosts,
Nameless in cardboard boxes, fading with them
On brittle, curling film, as one day I will fade.

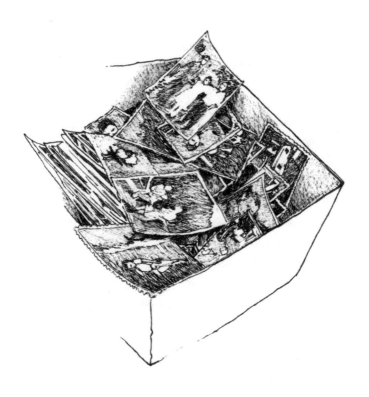

FRATER MEUS OCCISUS EST

In memoriam Murray Campbell

He left in the morning when no one was there,
In his undramatic, understated way,
As if it were all quite usual, no cause for concern,
As if unforced, as if by choice, as if in
    league with the tide.

A door closed, opened, it's hard to know which,
But beyond was a path, a road to the sea,
The red sun of dawn on the harbour waves,
Clouds on the peaks of well-remembered hills.

It was that time of year, the daffodils cleaving the earth,
The blossom biding its time,
Venus and Jupiter side by side,
Mars in a sulk in the south,
The birds deciding if this be the time to sing,
To gather moss, to fear the ice no more.

Away he sailed, and what was left we gave to
    the ground,
Planted him deep like a tree. On our shoulders we
    bore him,
We the men, his brothers and sons, taking all that
    was left,

Though nothing was left but the hollow husk,
The broken curves of a shell. We settled his roots in
    the chalk
Of the down, those breasted hills that were stretching
    their limbs,
Opened and heaped by the sexton's spade,
And pierced anew by the sword of spring.

We see him now, a golden flame in a boat ablaze,
Hand on the tiller,
Flaring up like a sun,
Flaming up with his own light on the further sea
With its own stars and its own moons,
Its unmapped shores and nameless winds.
I lower my eyes; my time will come;
Other tears will fall;
All will lie by another's side.
My brother, farewell,
My brother away with the breeze,
My brother in league with the tide.

WHAT MY MOTHER MEANS

1

Sausages cooked by Primus
On a chalky beach in Kent,
A sketch of St Michael's Mount.
Blue anorak, white wellies,
Furry mittens, pressed into my face.
Toboggans on the common.
Horse dung collected in a sack.
Golf and squash and tennis.
Sitting while I fished for hours
And never caught a fish.
Sermons and warnings
(Above all, and mostly, on sex).
Demands: Cut your hair, Be smart,
Get qualified, Get yourself a cosy little wife.
Advice: Don't worry, there's other fish in the sea,
Love is the most important thing;
The only way to be happy
Is making others happy.
There are many shades of grey.
Blackberries, rosehips in season,
Apples, daffodils and roses,

The dogged pursuit of slugs and snails,
Pruning, digging and turning,
Throwing the worms to a robin.
Evenings out at a play,
Long dresses for dinners.
Broken hearts for cats and dogs
Returned destroyed from the vet.
Sixty-five thousand, seven hundred meals.
Champagne, pink puddings, mince pies,
Pork with a peach on top, chicken Marengo,
Chocolate squidge, fruitcake, fudge.
Cocktail Sobranies, steak on Saturdays,
Boiled egg on Sundays,
Perfect pastry, fruity curry.
Praising her father,
Condemning the French,
Startling opinions,
Remembering school,
Remembering friends who died in the war.
Off to the WI, off to canvas for votes.
Sailing on the Solent,
Flowers and fruit, seeding, growing, arranging,
Creating a Garden of Peace,

3

Matt Munro, Jim Reeves, Ravel's *Boléro*.
Inherited wisdom;
There's so much good in the worst of us,
And so much bad in the best of us,
That it ill behoves any of us
To criticise the rest of us.
Great Moments: playing cricket for England,
Passing out first, the end of the war,
Pa's proposal,
Getting a freezer, getting a puppy,
Surfing by moonlight in Wales.

MY MOTHER, WHEN WE
COULD NOT SLEEP

My mother, when we could not sleep
In Mutti's house, would play piano,
Singing till we faded out, and fled,
And fused into the drifting fogs
Of dreams that hovered round our bed.

But when the house was given up,
The piano, too, was sold away,
And so my mother's music lived
Imprisoned in her hands, then starved,
And died of night, for lack of day.

MY MOTHER DYING

1

As the leaf on the bare branch, so my mother's ruined
   flesh
Is trembling for the earth;
To break off, to drift, to float down,
To settle and to crumble on the mould.

As the small bird who flies abroad
Flits from the bare branch and rises on the wind,
So does my mother's spirit, longing for the sun, flick
   its tail,
Bob its head, brace, leap, take off by instinct
To the far land unknown, unnamed, unknowable,
But urgently desired.

As the shipwrecked sailor, drifting for days,
Lets go at last of the floating spar,
So does my mother kick her pain away.

As the drowning creature begging for breath
At last inhales the bitter brine,
So does my mother, thirsting for help,
Breathe in death.

2

New moon and Jupiter, side by side,
Shoulder to shoulder, balanced above the waves,
Poised at the window, waiting in witness
To these, the last delays of her voyaging soul.
Then dawn at last; she opens her eyes.
'Look at the sea, sweet Mother, look at the sea,'
But my mother looks at the sky.
She closes her eyes, she breathes
Like one on a peak who climbs too fast too far.
On her behalf I gaze at the sea,
The boats on the skyline, the
Seabirds crying and wheeling.
I kiss her hands, I choke, I say last things,
And then it comes,
The final bate of breath, the gasp, the leaving.

MY MOTHER'S RINGS

We buried it with her, her wedding ring,
Worn down so thin by work, by time,
By stubborn, principled fidelity.
We kept it back, her wrecked engagement ring,
With missing diamond, scuffed ruby,
Its absent clasp, its band rubbed down to
The tenuous breadth of a thread.

I took it in to get it fixed. They said it
Was pointless, it's past repair.
We could take the stones and use them again –
But then, you know, it wouldn't be this ring.
This ring, they said, if washed, might fall apart.
This ring, they said, is kept intact by dirt.

This ring was lovely once; I loved its light,
When I was little, sparkling on her finger
With all the promise of marriage, the promise
Of one more ring, the one so worn we left it
On the wax digit of the waxen thing,
Got up in bridal white, that bore no resemblance,
That might have been someone else, but wore
My faithful mother's ring.

Christmas 2013

HER FATHER

He called her up at the time agreed, the usual hour on
   Sunday night.
He talked of the weather, he talked of the geese,
About to arrive on the same traditional day,
Honking over the house, rejoicing in sight of the marsh.

He said, 'Autumn is late this year.'

He paused so long she thought the line was down.
'I'm ninety-four,' he said at last, 'I'm tired, I've had
   enough, I'm off.'
Alarm and pain rose up in her throat
As, when the earth subsides, the water floods from wells.
'Would you like me to come?'
'No, don't worry. This dying is private stuff.'
'But Dad … '
'Don't worry. It's thousands of miles.
There's no need. I love you. See you in heaven, perhaps.
Enjoy the rest of your time.'

Three days passed, he took to his bed
And he flew out, as she and the geese flew in.

IN OCTOBER, TO MY FATHER

This cold October night is tracing patterns on the wall;
Shadows of the clouds are shifting strangely with the
    moon,
And there is no key to sleep.

Here I wait in autumn in the summer of my days,
A stranger in this city,
My thoughts my occupation and my prison.

I am thinking of my father;
The obscure debt,
The invisible hand that rests upon the shoulder.
The direct debt;
The flame of spirit dancing,
Within my body burning.

How small my harvest is;
There's little yet to offer, kneeling at his altar
With words the single fruit of all my learning.

Manchester 1974

FROM MY GREAT GRAND-MOTHER'S DIARY

Tight boots, went to Chislehurst, saw Empress Eugénie,
Tried to milk a cow, played bezique, Papa out to dinner,
Caught in hailstorm, drenched, saw Prince of Wales,
Papa home for dinner, attempted to make an omelette,
Street decorated for Czar, wrote to Papa, ducks' eggs
    stolen,
Played La Grace, won at draughts, strawberries, letter
    from Papa
To Mamma, Lucy and me, saw comet, Papa in town,
Made oatcakes and scones, croquet all by myself,
Lost my umbrella, went mushrooming, Papa home late,
Papa dining and sleeping in town, Papa gone off to
    Glasgow,
St Enoch's Hotel, danced, Papa home all day, skating
    with Papa,
Got no Valentine, not overwhelmed with grief,
Saw Duchess of Edinburgh, fell in love with Edith Price,
Lovely charming manners, lovely dark eyes, only nine
    years old,
Went to Chislehurst, saw Empress Eugénie and Prince
    Imperial,
Papa home to dinner, met him at the station, danced,
    read aloud,
Went to rink with Papa, did not go to church, sat on
    beach with Papa,

Made chocolate caramels, made chocolate creams, made
chocolate buns,
Went to dentist, beautiful moonlight, badminton till
dark, met Papa at Cannon Street,
Played billiards, walked out after dinner, Sophie fell in
the fire,
Had delicious ride on the thoroughbred, cut my hair
short,
Played cribbage and danced, played piquet with Papa as
usual,
Lost as usual, waltzed with Papa on the lawn.

MY YOUNG SELF

On the way home from the woods I met my younger
    self
And great pity seized my heart.
I was sorry for his muscled flesh, his unlined face,
The hot spark bright in his eyes, the chestnut hair,
The beautiful streak of blond,
The springstrong jaunt of his stride.

We exchanged greetings and I decided
To stay unknown. I wondered if he suspected.
His look was guarded, strange.
I said, 'Do you think you know me?'
'And why should I know you?' he said.

I looked at the trees, avoided his eyes.
The rooks above me hurled and flung in the wind.
I had so much to say, so much advice,
And so much sorrow for what would come.

'One day,' I said, 'you'll meet your younger self
On this same road, whilst wending home.
The rooks will wheel and call
In the Scots pines, in the ghosts of the elms.
There will be things, an infinite number of things
You'd like to say, but you'll walk on instead,

Back to your home in the woods,
Leaving your words, all your choice wise words,
All your sage advice, unsaid.'

FROG

She built a fire,
The frog was young,
The frog had never seen fire,
Had no fear of fire,
No instinctive knowledge, no experience,
No appreciation of any heat like fire.
The young frog saw
How pretty it was,
How fascinating,
How unlike anything else, and,
Before she could stop it,
It was too late, the frog had hopped.
The enlightened frog sat
Sizzling in wonder and awe, and
She put her hands to her face,
Undone, appalled, by unintended guilt.

ANTEROOM

Who are these people, walking in circles, sighing?

These are teenage celebrities, cadaverous ballerinas,
Stolid policemen, one-legged soldiers on crutches,
Infants in nappies and woolly booties,
Tourists with flux, and many more, infirm of purpose,
Some of whom have faces.

And on the doors of this room without walls
Are handwritten signs that read: ANTEROOM:
WAIT HERE TILL THE WAITING ENDS.

And they all wait, these people, walking in circles, sighing.

Yea, though they walk through the valley of the shadow
    of death,
They shall pay their parking fines,
Put cards in the meters,
Wash the dishes,
And even make love
With those who never say I love you;
But fritter their passionate hours in checking the time
On public clocks,
And thinking of how to clean the top-floor windows,
And how to prise the jackdaw nests from out of the
    chimneys

And finally saying 'I love you' when love's over,
When, at length, it all turned out to be biological,
And otherwise trivial.

On bleeding feet, the ballerina struggles home;
She'll sit and eat nothing, but smoke, to keep her figure
    neat.

And what are these doves, flying in circles?
They are not white doves
Or olive-bearing doves;
These are the doves that scrounge for bread
In the city squares,
Too timid to fly to the verdant fields where there's no
    bread,
But raw grain;
And are trapped by the squares and avenues and ledges,
And the kind old ladies, whose kindness and loneliness
Leave them dependent on doves
They have trapped in the squares,
These doves that are not white doves in holy, ineffable
    haloes of light,
But lame inedible doves that don't know why they live,
Aware that they have no choice
But to feed and mate and make more doves
For the kind old ladies who replaced the kind old ladies
There before,
In this succession of dying and kindness, kindness and
    dying,

This pathological hereditary generosity
Of those whose company has gone, and left them with
Shreds of memory; but otherwise
No company but whirling, scrounging, shabby flocks of
Unambitious birds.

And the kind old ladies feed these dislocated swarms
Amidst those who walk in circles, sighing;
The teenage celebrities, cadaverous ballerinas,
Unemployed actresses, builders in boots,
Pretty adolescents,
Would-be politicians, retired revolutionaries,
Stolid policemen, one-legged soldiers on crutches,
People who came from the office, and
Livid infants who throw themselves down and scream.

And on the doors of this room with invisible walls,
As large as the world,
Are handwritten signs that read: ANTEROOM:
WAIT HERE TILL THE WAITING ENDS.

IN DENTON CHURCHYARD (2)

Nothing here is harsh; the sun burns off the mist
That is the relic and reminder of the passing of the night.
Through limbs and leaves of trees
The new-made rays diffuse their tender golden light.
The day's reborn, the land draws in its breath; the robin
    sings,
The chaffinch and the wren.
The rooks hurl, the snowdrops lean against the breeze.

I've sworn to do my duty to the dead,
To taste the world on their behalf,
Swill it about my tongue, drink the liquor down.

You should have seen this dawn,
This dew, this new sun pale and bright,
Father, mother, lover, child, you beneath this soil,
Beyond the reach of torment or delight.

IN HAMBLEDON CHURCH-YARD, THE GRAVE OF LUCY PARKER

I saw your stone and stood appalled,
Here in the Surrey Hills,
With heaven so close, it's but a pace
From where I stand, one pace
From where you lie, my beauty, who,
When I was young, was far too young
To yearn for.

You barely lived out half a life,
Yet here you lie, Lucy, who was fifteen once,
And golden, lively, joyful, lovely,
Henceforth stilled and dumb.

This grave is eloquent with loss, a grief
That seeps up through the soil
And soaks the skin like dew.

Farewell to you,
So pristine once, so near to heaven,
Oblivious, in these Surrey Hills,
To those like me, who linger at this stone.

ANITA PALLENBERG IS
NEWLY DEAD

Anita Pallenberg is newly dead,
Long-lived beyond the bold fantastic age
When then she sparked with youth and loveliness,
And reckless, godless, self-destructive fun.

You golden woman, insolent and spoiled,
We longed for you, we envied you your self-
Made madness and your gilded cage,
Your shameless liberty, your sordid mess.

I watched an Irish blonde stroll by just now
And thought of you, and how it is that all
Our beauty flits from one, to one, to one.

I'll sit and wait here by this wrinkled sea,
Alert to those who have your beauty now,
This rare fine day of southern Dublin sun.

Dalkey 17/06/17

THE FORMER BEAUTY

The old woman knits for her friends,
Has people to stay,
Works in her garden, goes
Shopping in heavy-heeled shoes.

Asthma shortens her breath.
She groans as she stands,
The keys of the Bechstein remember no longer
The skip and dance of her hands.

Regard her well, read closely the lines of her face,
Perceive the life that lived in the eyes.
She who was loved by heroes,
Painted by artists, sculpted,
Feted by princes, posed for magazines,
Caused a poet to leap from a bridge,
A gallant lord to renounce his lands.

Who would have thought that here's where it ends?
She goes out for walks with a spaniel, embroiders
    cushions, like
Any old woman, knits colourful scarves for her friends.

INSIDE THEIR LOOSE CLOTHES

Inside their loose clothes, their chrysalis skin,
The old souls hide, of those who thought
That age would never come.

Their souls crouch down within, and wince
With pain, and pray for wings, and wait for sleep,
In order to be young again in dreams.

Inside their loose clothes and slackened skin
They wait for sleep that may, may not be birth.
Inside their shrunken world,
With patient dread, and,
Understanding nothing
But the need to fly or fall,
The old souls wait to go to earth.

DAYS OF LOVE AND REVOLUTION

Let's sing for the last time, Tovarisch,
Of the bright, abandoned days
Of Love and Revolution,
When comrades' names rolled off our tongues like
Rubies from a miser's hand; those
Innocent, unintelligent, youthful days
Of big ideas, impossible plans,
Implausible hopes, of slogans, red scrawls
On urban walls, and home-made flags;
When we were saviours of the world and champions of
The workers that we'd never met,
With whom, united, we'd never be defeated,
Who shook their heads and laughed us off,
And drowned their nights in beer.

We danced like puppets, fucked like rabbits,
But at greater length, with luck,
And with more finesse, so not
So much like rabbits, perhaps, and
I'd like to do so again; but how many times
Can you drink wine and eat bread
At the same communion, repeated
Ad infinitum
Till the light of the soul goes dull?

At night, asleep, I'm still a boy,
And it's only by day my belly sags
And the last grey hairs grow white,
And I ache if I sit too long.
And now my dreams are polluted by dismal things
I've been forced to learn since the
The days I had nothing to learn.

They've gone, Tovarisch, those bright,
Abandoned days of Love and Revolution,
But still I wait by the door
In case Love calls.
I'd hate to miss out when I'm in town
Or down at the doctor's
Or making a fire of sycamore leaves
In the corner down by the shed.

And as for you, My Lady,
My Mistress Revolution,
You've lost your beauty entirely;
You never were honest, saintly or holy.
I don't even spare you a thought
As I wait by the door for Love.

WE WHO WERE BORN TO
LIVE FOREVER

We who were born to live forever have now grown old;
Our joints lose faith, our hair is grey or gone,
Our hearts give out and cancers scythe us down.

But we were the golden hopeful ones
Who'd end the wars, make ploughs from guns.
We made love, played cheap guitars, knew three chords,
Considered our parents fascists, blamed society,
Took pompous music seriously, listened to gurus,
Compared star signs, consulted cards,
Smoked weed, looked for God in the smoke.

But we who were born to live forever have now grown old,
The joke was on us, those that survive.
How very beautiful, how sweet, how bright our eyes,
How quick and easy our answers,
How full of hope, how full of talk, how full of shit we were.

THE GREAT RADICAL

Of course I'm proud of my past! Regrets, I have none,
    almost none at all.
I did throw stones. As far as I know they always missed.
The bombs, well yes, but they never got used.
The petrol got put in the car, the bottles put out in the bin.

I wanted change, wanted to better the world, still do.
I haven't changed at all. I don't do demos and leaflets now,
But I never gave up my ideals.

And it's hardly my fault I won that prize for my book,
Sat on committees, enquiries, went on the box,
Got well paid, ended up in the Lords.

I didn't sell out, I'm still the same inside, the fire still burns.
I'm writing a book on social change, on what's to be done,
On what's gone wrong. They gave me a big advance.
I gave up bombs and stones; I'm still a terror with words.

NOT IN COFFEE SPOONS

This is how we measure our lives:

That was the year the old king died;

That was the year that Father was killed;

That was the year the dog
Was put out of its pain;

That was the year that mother went in
And never came out;

That was the year that war was declared
And the olives were scorched by frost;

That was the last occasion we met, we three,
And after that, were never together again.

Sisters, lovers, brothers, this is how it is:
We measure out our lives in lives lost.

THE JACK RUSSELL

He runs in the wake of the train,
Barking and chasing, barking and chasing;
Across the meadows and ditches
The small dog runs.
The train flees and the dog stops chasing,
Barking and chasing.
Always the winner, so fierce and swift and strong,
Once again, without dispute, he's won.
Pleased with himself, so proud and pleased,
He wags his stump and lifts his leg,
Sprinkles a tuft, a job well done.

THE LEGACY

I have a bank of drawers that store my long-held dreams,
My heart-close longings and desires,
Wrapped up in coloured tissue, neatly laid
In pretty rows, with labels stating what they are,
That name the year they were conceived,
That sometimes, even, nominate the day.

From time to time I take them out and clean them up,
These pretty baubles gathering tarnish,
With their patina of age, the cracks of shrinkage
As they dry, the deepened colours, beautiful,
But darker than they were. I keep them free of dust,
Against the day that might, but never seems to come.

I've left them to my children, this store of antique dreams,
That they might know their father as he was,
Not merely as he seemed to be, as Time devoured his
    time,
But as he always meant to be, when first he gathered
    dreams
And wrapped them up and cherished them, and laid
    them by in drawers,
Who wasn't built of meat and bone, but conjured up his
    own strange ghost
And formed himself from fantasy.

IN WHOM I DO NOT BELIEVE

1

I give thanks to God in whom I do not believe
For the land behind my home,
Where I am hunter-without-weapon in the hedgerows
    and spinneys;
Where, crouching silent, I await the mouse
Who sallies forth to sniff the air and wash its face,
Complacent on hind haunch outside the nest
Behind the hole no bigger than a coin
Between the roots of oak.

I give thanks to God in whom I do not believe
For the knowledge and the conversation of the birds
I name, who follow at a safe distance,
Demanding in urgent voices answers to questions
That are barely understood; and I tell them that
They are my free subjects, who pay me taxes
In strangeness and beauty, and whom I heap with
    honours,
Lords and ladies in their own manors.

2

I give thanks to God in whom I do not believe
For the dog who chases with no suspicion of futility

Deer I merely glimpse beside the burrow of the badger,
The mansion of the rabbit and the palace of the fox;
Where the sun fractures in splinters through the
Leaves of summer, and the very branches even in
The death of winter, when I read the night's activity
In sporemarks in the snow.

I give thanks to God in whom I do not believe
For the murky stream that is mire in autumn,
All but dry in summer, feeding standing pools
Where I confuse newts with dark fish, and panic ducks
Who yell their imprecations as they clatter past the
     trees,
Where fidget squirrels rain down husks of hazel,
Chittering and swearing at the snuffling dog
Who marks inconsequentially at toadstools in the
     moss.

3

I give thanks to God in whom I do not believe
For the island between two fields between two branches
     of a stream,
Impassable for fallen branches; and the rug of bluebells
I cannot bring my feet to crush, where, as a boy,
I was amazed by kingcups, by harebells, by the cycle
Of decay, by the silent owl who slept upon the
Bough above my head when all was still, and I, too,
Slept in broken sunlight by the banks awash with bees.

I give thanks to God in whom I do not believe
For the deer's skull found amid the stream;
For the dreams of the love of women unfolding
With the bud, when I was the first
And only boy amongst the tracks and burrows,
First Lord of Life and Duke of the Duchy
Of untrodden ways, and hummocks unexplained,
Except as breast and womb of the hidden God
In whom I do not believe,
Who milks my praise.

THE WAKE

Poor woman –
Crucifix in your right hand, rosary in your left,
Laid out rigid in your best blue gown,
Your chest razed flat where once your breasts had been.
How white your fingers are, how grey and blotched your
    face.
And, my love, your lips, so wide and full,
That should be living and kissing.
The wicker coffin, the Catholic candles,
Mother of God on the table, smug and still.
Poor woman, trusty servant of heaven,
Too much in love with the Lord,
Who thought you'd heal yourself through prayer,
Shat upon by God for all your forty-seven years.

LAZARUS

And when I rose, confused, from the cold stone slab,
Tight with windings, stinking of myrrh,
There loomed the Healer's face,
Still damp from tears, a face I'd loved
Since first I heard him preach, as
We shared our food in the trees' shade, in
A silver grove of olives, walled, with a well.

I'd known him all my life; we'd played together as boys.
I hadn't seen him for years, a prophet now in his own
    land!
I was, I know, an idle, flippant, superfluous man.
Some hoped he'd drive the pagans out; a magus, others
    said.
But as for me, I went in idleness; I had a friend grown
    famous,
And liked to hear what sophists say, what vagrant
    teachers teach.

Caught by surprise, I went to death unwillingly, it's true;
But now I'll live, perhaps grow old,
Compelled anew to weakness, fear and pain,
Remembering nothing from my dreamless,
Absent days, decaying in the cave.

Master, some years hence, perhaps, or soon,

In the self-same fetid hole,
Once more I'll stretch upon that hard, cold slab,
Tight with windings, stinking of myrrh.

Master, alas for your tender, misplaced love!
Master, alas for me, whom you raised up,
Perturbed once more by the old dread,
Condemned a second time to drain that dreadful cup.

Have pity, Lord, on Lazarus, twice dead.

MESSAGE TO SATAN

I'll send no news nor ask you how you are;
No doubt it's stark and cold in such black light,
No doubt you haven't changed at all. I'm keen
To know the reason you stay obstinate and mad.

And furthermore, I thought you'd like to know
I've angrily complained to God above
(Since He's the Chessman, mover of us all),
Demanding – as I ask from you – to know
What kind of love His is, that isn't love.

KLIO OF RHODES

Within this tomb lie slender bones,
Those of Klio of Rhodes, the former beauty,
Regretted by many, but not by wives,
Retired and expired in Kalymnos;
Who bequeathed to the Goddess the tools of her trade,
Along with her portrait, deftly done in lieu of cash
By Charmis of Kos, who perfectly captured her
    impudent smile,
Depicting in one hand a phallus,
A column of coins in the other.

To those who'd loved her skills, she left weak hearts
And empty pockets, wistful memories, aching muscles,
Various itches and rashes.

Her lyre and verses she left to Apollo.
Her lifetime's wealth she left to those she loved:
Her ancient cook, her Nubian slave, a girl she bought
In Crete, the cats she found in Samos,
Six or seven brindled dogs, her goat,
Her impotent husband, her many-fathered children.

LETTER TO AFRODITE
PHILOMEDA

There's been no news of you for fifteen hundred
    years.
We're wondering how you are. What mischief do you
    make
Out of the headlines, lovely slut of heaven? Have you
Lately loved a shepherd or slipped the grasp of Zeus?
And does your jaunty scallop shell still bear you up?
Your tranquil pool restore your often-lost virginity?
And how's your lame Hephaestus? Whose armour does
    he make?
And has he caught you out again?
And what attracted you to him?
We'd like to hear your news
Now that your statues are broken,
Their foreheads carved with crosses,
Your temples tumbled, rewrought into churches,
Stocked with everything you're not; those women
With their hair concealed in modest scarves, their
Babies not one whit as mischievous as yours.

We wonder how you are.
There's never been a time when you were needed
    more.
Be sure; one day we'll pay you back in lovers' tears.

We miss you, slut of heaven, mount your shell, come
    sailing home,
With swaying hips, and flowing hair.
There's been no news of you for fifteen hundred years.

KERKIRA

His skin hurts; it is tight and dark.
His body prickles from the salt and sun.
His blood is up, but there is no woman here
That he might serve, who might make use
Of all his lust and love.
The stars are brighter than the lamps; the swallows dip
  for flies,
The waves grind with a sound like distant wars.
There is music where the young ones dance
Their mime of lust and love.
There are lights blinking, dogs that howl to the yellow
  moon,
Crickets that grate in the vines, a horse that munches
  beneath the olives,
A dainty cat that begs for fish, perceives his sympathetic
  heart.
There's a yellow moon, a truce with fate,
Wine that glistens in the glass, swallows breasting the
  pool,
The sound of distant celebration, sailboats creaking,
Peace and calm at last, a place to meditate and wait,
Asylum on this island, hidden by the Greeks.

HAVENS

I set out on a voyage on the high seas
And anchored in many harbours.

In one they bade me worship many gods
In others they offered to kill me if I did.

In one place they bade me worship one god only
And in two others they told me the self-same thing,
But disagreed about His name
And told me I must kill the devils
Who thought His name was not The Name.

In two of these ports they said you can't eat pigs
And in one of those they killed my dogs
And broke my jars of wine,
And in another they said, 'You must drink wine –
It's the blood of God and His body is bread
And it's fine to be that kind of cannibal.'

And then I sailed to a strange place
Where they bade me worship no God,
Because there is no God,
And instead they worshipped tawdry things
That replaced God and in that manner
Were a pantheon of gods.

In all these ports the Books of God
Meant anything the faithful
Expected them to mean.

In the end, after many disappointing journeys
And threatening situations,
I said, 'God damn you all!' and hoisted sail
And sailed back out on the high seas,
Where God is in the wind
And the air of the soul is clean.

BUDDHA ON PRINCES STREET

He crouches on the grey stone step, this sunshrunk
    tramp,
With greasy cap and matted locks, who holds himself
In Perfect Posture, all his face a map of broken veins,
His eyes tight closed, his grimy hands at rest;
And by his feet, his life, his plastic bags, his bowl that
    holds five coins,
His hand-scrawled HOMELESS AND HUNGRY HELP,
His sleeping bag, his well-fed, well-brushed, well-loved
    dog.

The sun's come out of hiding, everyone's surprised;
The happy tourists stream up Castle Hill.

His memories have raised him up, have climbed
And made a woodbine with his fantasies and dreams.
He might have been a sailor once,
Had pretty bairns, been chucked out by the wife.
His eyes stay closed, his breathing slow; it seems
He's grasped the arcane alchemy that spins to gold
The salty jetsam of a wildly navigated life.

The sun's come out of hiding, such sweet heat;
The happy tourists stream up Castle Hill.

It's six coins now. His eyes stay closed. We do not think
To ask some explanation of his happiness,
Some stoned approximation to the truth.
He's gone from here, his vagrant soul is wheeling high,
And soaring with the sparkling gulls,
His bold heart beating to the distant drum,
The glinting promise of his lovely youth.

The sun's come out of hiding, pipes start up;
The happy tourists stream up Castle Hill.

BELFAST, AT THE END OF THE TROUBLES

By cloud and black hill the princess sleeps,
By quiet cold water.
Her soft grey eyes, her fine white skin,
Are dull beneath the dust,
Cobweb and broken brick,
Rusted iron and cracked tile,
Brass heart, knuckled hand and idle crane.
By cloud and black hill the princess sleeps,
Unkissed, by quiet cold water.
She has dreamed of dragons that grew too real.
But light breaks and she wakes at last,
Smiling, and astonished by her long sleep's tears.

INNOCENT MEN ON BISHOP'S QUAY

In Limerick down by the river,
A lamp post told me to pick up after my dog.
I put him right.
I said, 'Listen lamp post,
Think before you speak.
I'm English, I've got two cats
And they're not keen on travel.'

But the lamp post was undeterred,
And said the same thing
In the same tone of voice
To the man who came after,
Who was certainly Irish,
But also had no dog,
And was just as vexed as me.

MANCHESTER, ON A DAY OF EXTREME HEAT IN THE 1970S

Summer squats on Manchester,
Leans against its chest,
Its fingers at the throat.
A mist of dust in the evening air
Sprinkles all the sunset on the city
Like a fountain.
In humidity and humility
A thousand reeking chimneys seep amongst the spires
Their sooty meditations.

The workers stream with rivulets
That glisten through the grime upon their shoulders;
They shake away the pearls of sweat
That glow upon their eyelids
Or glimmer on their foreheads like the opal.

Unfortunate city, drowsy as a hive,
Barely breathing, thirsty as a slave,
City of a thousand aspirations,
Longing only at this moment
For the old familiar rain.

SEVILLANAS

When the sun snags in the orange trees,
Then the young girls dance flamenco in Seville.
The man in the square, guitar perched high,
And eyes pinched tight,
Pours out his joys and his accumulated griefs,
And rasps the Sevillanas.

The grim cathedral disapproves,
The priests don't watch,
But cabmen's horses prick their ears
And prance and step out proud.

They love it as I love it,
When the young girls dance.

TURKISH COUPLE WITH A
LIONITIS CHILD IN FETHIYE

Bravely they sauntered, hand in hand,
The little one between.
Slowly they went, their shoulders square,
The fish jumping, the flies hatching.
The imam switched on the azan,
But they strolled beside the canal,
Hands in the hands of their hideous girl,
Who couldn't live long. They were not
Ashamed, they were parents who loved their child.

ON IPANEMA BEACH

The brown people, the black people,
The almost white people,
Immortal boys, the soft-hipped girls,
The lovers of the sand,
Children suckled at the breast of coconut,
Gold and gleaming,
Applaud the maestro sun,
Who takes his bow,
And sinks between two rocks,
And leaves behind
Another virtuoso day.

IN KATHMANDU

Dead hog in the river,
Caught up on a pile of the bridge,
Swollen and stinking, festooned with litter,
Painted in filth,
Marooned in the Holy River,
Coated with Hindu dead,
This trickling mud,
Gleaming and grey,
This Holy River,
Thick with the ash of the ghats.

LAST YEAR

Last year we met among the trees
And lay down in the flowers.

Those flowers have bloomed again
And new leaves bud on the bare boughs
Of the same trees.

I think of how my body fails,
Of how I lay in other fields with other loves,
Of how the world has been my bed.

You shouldn't have said you might return one day.
I'm vagrant now in my own house.
I waste whole days at the window.

I wonder how many times the sun must set,
The moon rise, the seasons turn,
The stars revolve, about this house.

It seems unjust, and I should be ashamed,
That spring should make me sad,
When last year we met amongst the trees
And lay down in the flowers.

I'M GOING BACK INTO THE GARDEN

I'm going back in the garden, for this is the season you
    wandered off.
I'd like to see if spring will bring you back.

This garden was ravaged by winter, I think the fig tree's
    dead.
The tulips, at least, were secure in the mould.

This garden was Paradise once, but then the rose fell sick,
The vines grew mean, the wind burned out the leaves.

I sang to the beeches, 'Your boughs are dishevelled,
You've lost your pride. I'll drink your health in wine.'

My mind was tortured once, but now my strength's
    returned,
Enough to lift a jug, break bread and dig.

I'm going back in the garden, to clear some space for the
    rugs,
My lutes and lanterns, pillows and bowls of fruit.

All these jubilant songbirds, I wish I knew their names.
I'd send them cards, inviting them to sing, should you
    return.

IN THE WOODS NEAR
SWEETWATER

This soft turf, this dark peat
Composed of leaves and fallen trees,
Is the same turf I walked with her
In the awkward days of greatest strength,
When we were lovely, barely formed,
Yet never better formed, and
Never more aflame,
Never faster carried off by
The disingenuous lying promise of life.

I remember a rusted car,
Bracken as high as our heads,
A hurtling dog with a branch in his jaws,
Anxious to fetch, anxious to please,
A silent lake, a quarry of sand,
A tunnel of rhododendron.

We were poor at conversation,
Poor at holding hands,
Poor at love, frightened of love,
That love constrained by buckles and bars.

I swear she was fashioned of velvet,
Cinnamon, honey of thyme.
Her voice was warm and low.

I swear she was formed by a mischievous god
Giving me something to aim for,
Something to fall short of,
An apple I could not grasp,
A summit I could not reach.

As wasps and mould devour the damsons,
Small and sweet and wild,
Scattered in these woods like words,
So all our days have been devoured,
That tumbled from the branches,
Like unsuspecting birds.

IN MY OWN HOUSE

I passed you by in my own house;
I was one of the fittings – inventory –
Something large that moves.
I restrained my hands, withheld my touch,
The kiss, the loving word.
I was drifting merely, from one solitude
At this end of my own house,
To a further one at the other,
Demoted from lover to bursar,
Convenient but inconvenient,
An indentation in your paragraph,
Space in your double spacing,
Tangible ghost in my own house,
Sleeping apart in the same bed,
Loved by others outside,
Dulling with dust in a corner.
They darken and tighten, my tarnishing strings
My timbers unglue in the damp
At one end of my own house.
You at the other, the music dead in your heart.

AN INCOMPATIBILITY

It wasn't her tawny, sunwarmed flesh that put him off,
Nor her long, entwining limbs, her admirable skills
With hand and mouth and tongue; nor
Her fascinating conversation, her sympathetic heart;
Nor her willingness to move a thousand miles,
Forsake her land and give up everything.

It was that she sang so badly, her voice was thin and small,
And he was all musician, music was the most part of his
    world.

Her intonation made him wince;
He couldn't bear it, the keylessness, the breathiness,
The pauses wrongly placed, the notes held on
Or cut too short, that made him long to put
A pistol to his tortured head and black it out,
Her execrable singing.

SHE LAID SIEGE

She brought me gifts of eggs and cakes,
Drank tea and laughed, and sympathised,
And paid attention to my righteous tales.

And then,
With teams of bullocks and horses,
In the owl-lapped dead of night,
She dragged up ballistas, catapults, towers,
Lethal engines of war.

One day at dawn, while I still slept,
As frightened larks fled up from the heath,
As buzzards gathered above the fields
And rats licked their lips in the ditches,
She came upon me slowly, bold beneath
Her sturdy tortoise of shields.

And last, most fatal of all,
She made a tunnel beneath the moat,
Beneath my ribs, a fathom deep,
Below the footings of my stubborn heart,
And broke the stones and sapped the walls,
And undermined my well-kept keep.

SHE WAS PLAYING SCHUBERT

I remember you best
When you were twenty,
Clothed in nothing but
Your waterfall of hair.
Your locks were black,
Cascading to your waist.
Your arms were white as moonlight.
You were very petite.
There was nothing about you
A painter would have changed.

It was summer;
All the windows were open
Like welcoming arms,
And you were playing Schubert,
Naked before the piano,
Your delicate fingers teasing the keys.

Your impudent purity
Silvered the room,
And all your life was before you.

King's Lynn 2017

BLACKBIRDS AND ROBINS

I saw blackbirds and robins this morning
And thought of you,
She wrote from her office in town,
To me in my home in the wilds.
I wondered what to make of this;
Such a phantom stroke on the cheek,
Such a distant kiss.